THE BOOK OF
SAINTS

Paul Harrison

WAYLAND
www.waylandbooks.co.uk

First published in 2017 by Wayland
Copyright © Wayland 2017

Editor: Sarah Silver
Designer: Elaine Wilkinson

ISBN HB 978 1 5263 0186 4

Printed in China

10 9 8 7 6 5 4 3 2 1

MIX
Paper from responsible sources
FSC® C104740
www.fsc.org

aSuruwataRi/Shutterstock: 22.aSuruwataRi/Shutterstock: 22. Zvonimir Atletic/Shutterstock: 2t, 12t, 16, 26, 30. bogdb/istockphoto: 17t. Joaquin Ossorio Castillo/Shutterstock: 10b. Chrispo/Shutterstock: 8bc. Danileon/Dreamstime: 27b. Keith Dannemiller/Alamy: 5t. DEA/Seemuller/Getty Images: 18. fototeca gilardi/Marka/Superstock: 28t. Fotomy/Dreamstime: 19. Maran Garai/Shutterstock: 13r. Granger NY/Alamy: 10t. Sonia Halliday Library/Alamy: 29. Hchc2009/wikimedia commons: back cover bl, 14l. Birgit Reitz-Holman/Shutterstock: 5c. Kevin Holt/istockphoto: front cover tl, 25. ilbusca/istockphoto: 6t. Jurand/Shutterstock: 1t, 11t. Francois Lochon/Gamma/Getty Images: 7t. Stephen Puliafico/Dreamstime: 28b. Anna Rassadnikova/Shutterstock: back cover br, 1bl, 2b, 5b, 6b, 8bc, 11b, 13b, 14b, 17b, 21b, 23b, 26b, 31b, 32. Jozef Sedmak/Dreamstime: 3, 8l, 15t, 21t, 24. Renata Sedmakova/Shutterstock: 4, 20. Striking Images/Alamy: 23t. Thoom/Shutterstock: 1br, 23c, 31t. Tupungato/Dreamstime: front cover tr. Ullsteinbild/Getty Images: 9. Vatican Pool/Getty Images: 7b. Edward Westmacott/Dreamstime: 12b. CC Wikimedia Commons: back cover t, 27t. Zvonimir Atletic/Shutterstock: 2t, 12t, 16, 26, 30. bogdb/istockphoto: 17t. Joaquin Ossorio Castillo/Shutterstock: 10b. Chrispo/Shutterstock: 8bc. Danileon/Dreamstime: 27b. Keith Dannemiller/Alamy: 5t. DEA/Seemuller/Getty Images: 18. fototeca gilardi/Marka/Superstock: 28t. Fotomy/Dreamstime: 19. Maran Garai/Shutterstock: 13r. Granger NY/Alamy: 10t. Sonia Halliday Library/Alamy: 29. Hchc2009/wikimedia commons: back cover bl, 14l. Birgit Reitz-Holman/Shutterstock: 5c. Kevin Holt/istockphoto: front cover tl, 25. ilbusca/istockphoto: 6t. Jurand/Shutterstock: 1t, 11t. Francois Lochon/Gamma/Getty Images: 7t. Stephen Puliafico/Dreamstime: 28b. Anna Rassadnikova/Shutterstock: back cover br, 1bl, 2b, 5b, 6b, 8bc, 11b, 13b, 14b, 17b, 21b, 23b, 26b, 31b, 32. Jozef Sedmak/Dreamstime: 3, 8l, 15t, 21t, 24. Renata Sedmakova/Shutterstock: 4, 20. Striking Images/Alamy: 23t. Thoom/Shutterstock: 1br, 23c, 31t. Tupungato/Dreamstime: front cover tr. Ullsteinbild/Getty Images: 9. Vatican Pool/Getty Images: 7b. Edward Westmacott/Dreamstime: 12b. CC Wikimedia Commons: back cover t, 27t.

Disclaimer: Every effort has been made to trace the copyright holders but if you feel you have the rights to any images contained in this book, then please contact the publisher.

A cataloguing record for this title is available at the British Library.

Wayland, an imprint of Hachette Children's Group
Part of Hodder & Stoughton
Carmelite House
50 Victoria Embankment
London EC4Y 0DZ

An Hachette UK Company
www.hachette.co.uk
www.hachettechildrens.co.uk

CONTENTS

WHAT IS A SAINT?

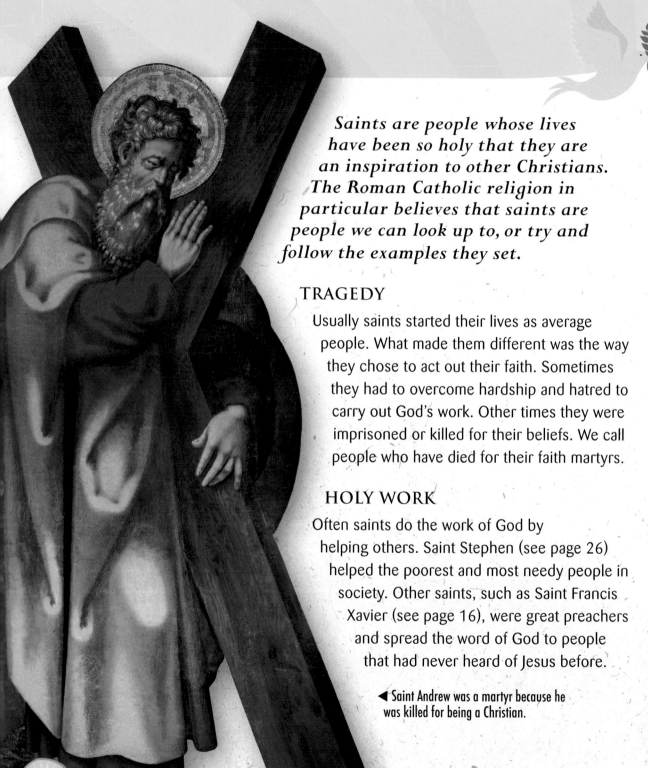

Saints are people whose lives have been so holy that they are an inspiration to other Christians. The Roman Catholic religion in particular believes that saints are people we can look up to, or try and follow the examples they set.

TRAGEDY

Usually saints started their lives as average people. What made them different was the way they chose to act out their faith. Sometimes they had to overcome hardship and hatred to carry out God's work. Other times they were imprisoned or killed for their beliefs. We call people who have died for their faith martyrs.

HOLY WORK

Often saints do the work of God by helping others. Saint Stephen (see page 26) helped the poorest and most needy people in society. Other saints, such as Saint Francis Xavier (see page 16), were great preachers and spread the word of God to people that had never heard of Jesus before.

◄ Saint Andrew was a martyr because he was killed for being a Christian.

▲ Sometimes statues
of saints are carried during
religious celebrations.

Some people, called missionaries, travel great distances
to do God's work. Sometimes these men and women
inspired people so much with the holiness of
their lives that they were declared saints after
their death.

FEAST DAYS AND PATRONS

Saints are remembered on days called
feast days. Christians often pray to
saints, asking for help or guidance.
This is especially true if that saint is
a patron, which means having a special
connection to the thing the person is praying
about. For example, people who are about to
make a journey might pray to Saint Christopher,
as he is the patron saint of travellers.

▲ People travelling might
carry a pendant showing
Saint Christopher.

HOW TO BECOME A SAINT

▲ Pope Gregory IX

There are over 10,000 saints that we know of today. Many are from the earliest days of Christianity, a few hundred years after Jesus's death. Often we don't know very much about these people, but their stories have been passed down through history. Many of these saints were martyred for their faith. Saints are still being made today.

CHANGING RULES

There used to be no real rules about who could be a saint. Generally, people who had lived holy lives (for example by following the 10 commandments) or who had been martyrs, were declared saints soon after their death. Things changed in 1234. Pope Gregory IX made a rule that before anyone could be declared a saint there had to be an investigation into that person's life to see if they deserved the title of saint. Since then, the rules have changed a number of times until the Church arrived at the process it has today.

▶ Mother Teresa lived a very holy life, helping the sick and poor, particularly in Kolkata, India.

MIRACLE MAKERS

The first step in the process is to investigate the life of the person who has died to make sure they lived in a holy enough way. The next step is to see if a miracle – a happy or good turn of events that cannot be explained by science – has taken place in the person's name. This means that someone has prayed to the person for help and a miracle has occurred. In the case of Mother Teresa, someone who was ill prayed to her and her illness unexpectedly went away. When a miracle happens the person is said to be beatified or blessed.

THE FINAL STEP

If another miracle has been proven to have happened then the person can be canonised – which means they become a saint. Usually this process takes around five years, but in the case of Mother Teresa it was much shorter. This happened because the two miracles that occurred (both were people recovering from illness), happened soon after her death, so the Catholic Church was happy to canonise her earlier than expected.

◀ Pope Francis has canonised over 30 saints, including Mother Teresa on 4 September 2016.

Died:
Around CE 60

Feast Day:
30 November

Patron saint of:
Scotland and Russia

Saint
ANDREW

Saint Andrew was the brother of Saint Peter and was one of the first apostles. Andrew is often mentioned in the Bible; but in many ways it was what happened after he died that is more interesting.

The Bible tells us that Andrew came from the town of Capernaum on the shores of the Sea of Galilee in what is now modern-day Israel. Like his brother he worked as a fisherman, until he became one of Jesus's apostles. He went out to preach the word of Jesus before he died for his faith by being crucified on an X-shaped cross. His body was buried in a place called Patras in Greece.

Legend has it that his remains were then taken on a holy tour around Europe. It is claimed that they even came as far north as Scotland, which is why this martyr from Capernaum became the patron saint of Scotland, thousands of miles from where Saint Andrew lived!

▼ The national flag of Scotland is a white X-shaped cross on a blue background.

Saint ANSGAR

Right up until the 1800s, hardly anyone went on holidays, and venturing beyond the nearest town was rare. This makes the journeys taken by early Christian missionaries like Saint Ansgar even more remarkable.

Ansgar was born in France in 801. He became a monk and moved to Germany, where he became Archbishop of Hamburg. However, the area was attacked by Vikings who destroyed the town and burned down the church. While most people tried to stay clear of these fearsome warriors, Ansgar went to Sweden and Denmark where the Vikings came from, in an attempt to make them Christians.

Ansgar impressed the people with his good deeds and the schools he set up. He also worked hard to stop the Vikings using slaves. When he died he was buried in Bremen in Germany.

Lived:
801–865

Feast Day:
3 February

Patron saint of:
Scandinavia

◄ Ansgar is often depicted holding a model church to represent his work as a missionary.

Saint BERNADETTE

Saint Bernadette was 14 years old and working as a shepherd when she saw a vision of the Virgin Mary in the mouth of a cave. A spring of water began to flow and Mary told Bernadette to build a church on the site.

▲ Bernadette joined an order of nuns called the Sisters of Charity.

Bernadette saw Mary around eighteen times in a place called Massabielle near Lourdes, in France. At first people didn't believe her; but Bernadette stuck to her story and won people over with her honesty and integrity. People began to flock to the area and to bathe in the water, believing it was holy and it would cure them of various illnesses.

Lived:
1844–1879
Feast Day:
16 April
Patron saint of:
Ill people

However, Bernadette never saw the visitors or the church. By the time the church had been built she had moved away and become a nun, living the quiet, holy life she wanted. She died at the young age of 35 and was made a saint 50 years later.

◀ Today, millions of people visit Lourdes every year and pray in the church that was built as Saint Bernadette reported Mary wished.

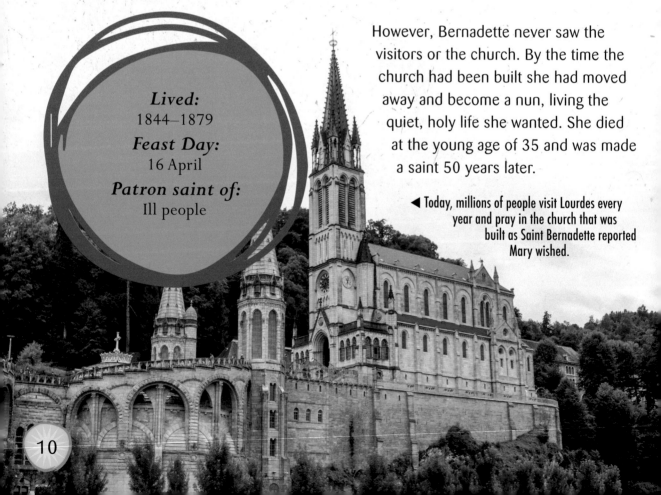

Saint
BRIGID OF KILDARE

Often, the less we know about a saint the more amazing the stories that have grown about them. Saint Brigid, an Irish slave who became a nun, is a good example.

▲ The curved stick on the right, called a crosier, is the symbol of a leader.

Lived:
Around 500
Feast Day:
1 February
Patron saint of:
Ireland

We know very few actual facts about Brigid's life – but there are lots of amazing myths and legends! Brigid may have been a slave, but she was known for her generosity, giving away whatever she had and also giving away the property of her master. The stories say that no matter how much she gave away, she never seemed to run out of what she gave, so her master could never punish her.

Other tales about her claim that, to avoid being married, she prayed that God would make her ugly to put people off. Apparently it worked and her beauty returned when she became a nun. It is said that Saint Patrick (see page 23), baptised Bridget and that she built a monastery at Kildare, in Ireland, to help spread Christianity.

Did You Know?
Saint Brigid is sometimes called Brigid the Fearless because she wasn't scared of anyone.

Saint
CATHERINE OF ALEXANDRIA

▲ Images of Saint Catherine often show the broken wheel that she was meant to die on.

In the early years of the first millennium, there were many martyrs, because having a different religion from the ruler in charge could get you killed. Many Christians were put to death. Saint Catherine was one of these martyrs.

Catherine was about 18 years old when she became a Christian. She converted at least 50 people to her new religion – including (it is said) some members of the Roman Emperor's family. The Emperor, a man called Maxentius, had her followers executed and condemned Catherine to die on a spiked wheel. However, the wheel shattered instead of killing her. It didn't spare Catherine, as she was beheaded instead, but people took the wheel as a sign of the power of Christianity.

Lived:
Around 300

Feast Day:
25 November

Patron saint of:
Philosophers and scholars

Did You Know?
We commemorate Saint Catherine every November 5th – the firework called the Catherine wheel is named in her honour.

Saint CHRISTOPHER

Saint Christopher is one of the most famous of all the saints. Today he is the patron saint of travellers. However he wasn't always such a helpful person — until he met a small child, that is.

It is thought that Christopher was from Canaan (in the modern-day Middle East) and he was said to be very tall and very strong. He wanted to serve the most powerful man around. This turned out to be an outlaw known as the Devil. But when the Devil turned out to be afraid of Christianity, Christopher decided to serve God instead.

Myth has it that he helped a small child to cross a river. The child was unbelievably heavy and when Christopher asked why, the child replied that he was Jesus and when Christopher carried him he also bore the weight of the world upon his shoulders. Early Christians gave him the name Christopher (which means Christ-carrier) and this is how we know him to this day.

Lived:
Around 200–300
Feast Day:
25 July
Patron saint of:
Travellers

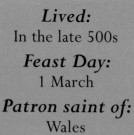

Lived:
In the late 500s

Feast Day:
1 March

Patron saint of:
Wales

Saint
DAVID

Saint David was the son of a Welsh king, but he turned away from his royal life to become a monk. He could have been king, but in his eyes he was serving a greater king in God.

David was born in Wales sometime in the 500s and became a monk – probably living in different monasteries in Wales and in England. The monks there lived very simple lives, drinking only water and eating only vegetables and bread.

David was such a great preacher that he was made archbishop. In one famous story the ground rose up under David's feet so people could see him preach. He worked mainly in the Pembrokeshire area of Wales, spreading the word of God. Today he is remembered on 1 March, known as Saint David's Day.

◀ Saint David is often shown with a dove to represent the Holy Spirit, which gave him the gift of good speech.

Did You Know?
Saint David was said to stand neck-deep in freezing water when he prayed as a punishment for anything he had done wrong.

▲ Saint Francis is often shown talking to animals.

Saint
FRANCIS OF ASSISI

Lived:
1181–1226

Feast Day:
4 October

Patron saint of:
Italy and ecology

Saints often find their lives are transformed when they try to follow the teachings of Jesus. This was certainly true of Saint Francis.

Francis was born in Assisi, Italy, where he grew up enjoying a life of privilege. But Francis gave all his money away to the poor and became a preacher instead.

At first, he often lived by himself and talked to animals as if they were his friends. Later, other men, impressed by Francis's holiness, began to help him in his work to serve God. These would become an order of monks known as the Franciscan friars (or brothers) – dedicated to living simply and giving to the poor.

According to a history of Saint Francis written in 1230, the saint received wounds to his hands, feet and side after seeing a vision of an angel in 1224. These wounds are known as stigmata and represent the wounds suffered by Jesus when he was crucified on a cross. The wounds disappeared at a later date as mysteriously as they had arrived.

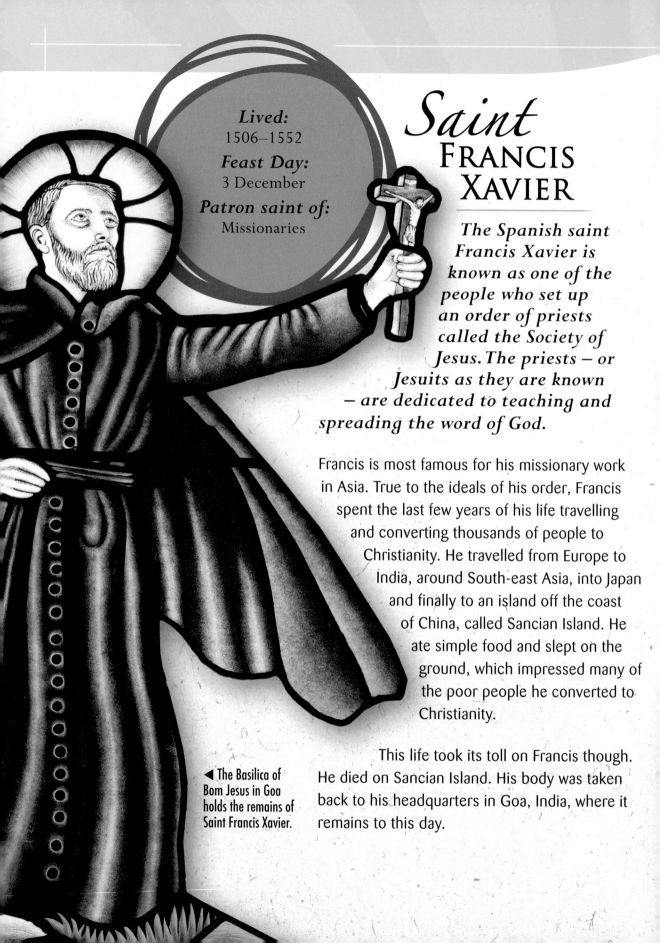

Lived:
1506–1552

Feast Day:
3 December

Patron saint of:
Missionaries

Saint
FRANCIS XAVIER

The Spanish saint Francis Xavier is known as one of the people who set up an order of priests called the Society of Jesus. The priests – or Jesuits as they are known – are dedicated to teaching and spreading the word of God.

Francis is most famous for his missionary work in Asia. True to the ideals of his order, Francis spent the last few years of his life travelling and converting thousands of people to Christianity. He travelled from Europe to India, around South-east Asia, into Japan and finally to an island off the coast of China, called Sancian Island. He ate simple food and slept on the ground, which impressed many of the poor people he converted to Christianity.

This life took its toll on Francis though. He died on Sancian Island. His body was taken back to his headquarters in Goa, India, where it remains to this day.

◀ The Basilica of Bom Jesus in Goa holds the remains of Saint Francis Xavier.

◀ Legends about dragons were popular during the Middle Ages.

Saint GEORGE

Saint George was probably a Roman soldier living in what is now Palestine. Although he is the patron saint of England, he never came to England, and may not even have heard of the country.

Died:
Around 303

Feast Day:
23 April

Patron saint of:
England

George became famous for a story that travelled all the way to northern Europe. The story is that George heard about a dragon that was terrorising a town. The locals would leave two sheep for the beast, but when they ran out of sheep they were forced to choose a person to be sacrificed. The King's daughter was picked, but George came to her rescue by killing the dragon – and the townsfolk became Christian in thanks for being rid of the monster.

Although people in Britain had heard of Saint George as early as the 700s, he really became famous during a series of wars through the Middle Ages between Christians and Muslims, called the crusades. The English soldiers would pray to Saint George and it is probably for this reason that he became the patron saint of England.

Saint
JOAN OF ARC

◄ It is amazing to think that a teenage girl led the French army.

During the early 1400s, France was at war with England. The English army had invaded and the French were losing, when a new leader changed their fortunes. But this leader wasn't a general or a king – it was a 15-year-old peasant girl called Joan.

Joan was only 14 when she claimed to hear God telling her to save her country. She found she was able to see what was going to happen in future battles, which brought her to the attention of the French leaders. They quizzed her for three weeks to see if she was telling the truth and when they were convinced she was, they chose her to lead the troops.

Joan led the army to rescue the town of Orléans and then in successful battles in the Loire region of France. However, she was captured the following year and was put to death by being burnt at the stake.

Lived:
1412–1431
Feast Day:
30 May
Patron saint of:
France

Did You Know?
Saint Joan is also known as the Maid of Orléans.

18

Saint
JOHN THE BAPTIST

Lived:
1st century

Feast Day:
24 June

Patron saint of:
Jordan and
Puerto Rico

John was a preacher who would baptise people if they believed in God. Baptising is symbolically washing away a person's past sins, or faults, by pouring water over them.

John's message was that the Messiah, or saviour, was coming and people should be prepared. Then one day John saw the man he had been preaching about come to be baptised – it was Jesus. John and Jesus were actually related and had known each other since they were children. However, when Jesus appeared that day, John realised that Jesus was the Son of God. John told his followers that they should listen to what Jesus preached from then on.

However, the local ruler, Herod, was upset by what John said about Jesus. He had John arrested, and worse was to come. Herod's daughter, Salome, impressed Herod with her dancing on his birthday. He promised her anything she wanted – she asked for John the Baptist's head. True to his word, Herod ordered John to be executed immediately.

◄ In some countries, Saint John the Baptist's feast day is a public holiday.

Saint JUDE

Jude is the patron saint of hopeless cases, which means he is the saint people pray to when it feels like there is no other hope.

Lived:
1st century

Feast Day:
28 October

Patron saint of:
Hopeless cases

When people think of Saint Jude they often get him mixed up with someone else completely. Partly this is down to the fact that Jude is also known as Saint Thaddeus. However, the name Jude is also similar to Judas, so people get the saint confused with the apostle who betrayed Jesus.

Saint Jude may have been chosen as the patron of hopeless cases as a result of his unpopularity, due to the confusion between himself and Judas.

Jude was one of the 12 apostles and was the brother of James, who was also an apostle. It is thought that Jude travelled around the Middle East preaching, before being put to death for being a Christian. It is also believed that he is buried in Rome alongside Saint Peter.

◄ Saint Jude is often shown with or wearing a picture of Jesus.

▲ The four gospel writing saints are known as the evangelists.

Saints
MATTHEW, MARK, LUKE AND JOHN

Lived:
1st century

Feast Day:
Matthew – 21 September
Mark – 25 April
Luke – 18 October
John – 27 December

Patron saint of:
Matthew – Bankers
Mark – Lawyers
Luke – Doctors
John – Friendship

These four saints are usually grouped together because they wrote the stories about Jesus that we call the gospels.

The gospels were put together to make what is called the New Testament stories of the Bible and they are how we know about Jesus today.

Saints Matthew and John were two of Jesus's apostles, so they saw what they were writing about with their own eyes. Saints Mark and Luke lived and talked with people who had seen and knew Jesus to get the information for their gospels.

Patron saint of:
Police officers, doctors
and grocers

Saint MICHAEL

To be a saint you have to be a good person – but you don't have to be human!

Saint Michael is an angel. In fact, he is an archangel, which means he is one of the chief angels, sent by God as a messenger when there is something important to be done. The idea of creatures like angels and archangels exists in different religions around the world. Saint Michael is one of only three archangels mentioned in the Bible (the other two are Raphael and Gabriel, who are also the only other saints who are angels).

Saint Michael has two roles: the first is as the leader of God's army of angels that stand ready to do battle with the Devil. Saint Michael is often shown fighting against a huge dragon, which represents evil. It is said that Michael's other job is to escort the souls of the dead up to Heaven. People have prayed to Saint Michael for help since the early 400s, which is one of the reasons he became known as a saint.

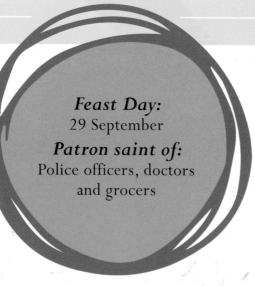

▼ Saint Michael is often shown wearing armour or carrying a sword.

Lived:
Around 390–461
Feast Day:
17 March
Patron saint of:
Ireland

▲ Today, Saint Patrick's feast day is celebrated with parades – especially in Dublin, Ireland and New York in the USA.

Saint PATRICK

Sometimes amazing stories start with the most unlikely of beginnings. This is certainly true of Saint Patrick – the story of how a slave became a bishop and converted a country to Christianity.

▲ Saint Patrick used the three-leafed shamrock plant to explain the idea of the holy trinity.

Did You Know?

It is said that Patrick once preached for so long that his walking stick took root in the ground and grew into a tree.

Patrick was born and raised in either Scotland or Wales, but when he was 16 years old he was captured by Irish pirates and sold as a slave. He spent the next six years working as a shepherd for an Irish ruler. He managed to escape back to Britain where he trained to be a priest.

In 435 he returned to Ireland; not as a slave but as a Christian missionary – someone who preaches to people of a different, or no, religion. He became bishop and converted a lot of the country by using simple ways of explaining his faith.

Saint
PAUL

Of all the stories of saints who have become better people, none can rival the change that overcame Saint Paul. He was a man who went from persecuting Christians to being a Christian martyr himself.

Saint Paul used to be known as Saul. He hated Christians and may well have been in charge of the stoning to death of Saint Stephen (see page 26). One day, when Saul was travelling to a place called Damascus, a blinding light knocked him from his horse and he heard a voice asking why he was persecuting God.

Saul was blinded for three days. He realised the mistakes he had made, was baptised a Christian and his sight returned. He changed his name to Paul to symbolise his new start and went on three missions around the Middle East and Greece to spread the Christian message. He was martyred in Rome.

▲ Stained glass depicting Saul being blinded by God.

Died:
Around CE 67
Feast Day:
29 June
Patron saint of:
Writers

Died:
CE 64

Feast Day:
29 June

Patron saint of:
Fishermen

Saint PETER

Saint Peter was a fisherman who became Jesus's most trusted apostle and eventually the head of the Christian faith.

Peter was originally called Simon, but Jesus changed his name to Peter. The name Peter means 'rock' and Jesus told Peter that he would be the rock on which his new religion would be built.

Peter did not always find it easy being one of the apostles. When the time came to prove his loyalty to Jesus, Peter failed. When Jesus had been arrested and was about to be put to death, Peter denied that he was an apostle – not once, but three times! Jesus forgave him and Peter never lacked the courage to be open about his faith again.

Peter led the apostles after Jesus ascended to Heaven and was the first apostle to perform a miracle. It was Peter who allowed gentiles (non-Jewish people) to join them. He travelled to Rome where he was crucified for being a Christian and is said to be buried under the Vatican.

◄ Saint Peter is often shown holding the keys to Heaven.

Died:
CE 35

Feast Day:
26 December

Patron saint of:
Bricklayers

Saint
STEPHEN

To have the courage to die for what you believe in is the biggest sacrifice that a person can make. Saint Stephen was the first person to be killed for their Christian beliefs when he was stoned to death for preaching about his religion.

Stephen was given the job of deacon by the apostles. Being a deacon meant that Stephen was responsible for giving money raised by Christians to people who were in need. Stephen also talked to people about Jesus.

When the Jewish authorities heard what Stephen was saying they accused him of blasphemy, which means being disrespectful about God. Stephen spoke with great passion and courage about what he believed in, but was immediately taken away and stoned to death. It is said that Saul (later Saint Paul, see page 24) helped organise his death.

▲ The palm leaf Saint Stephen carries is a symbol of martyrdom.

Did You Know?
Boxing Day (the day after Christmas Day) is also called Saint Stephen's Day because that is the saint's feast day.

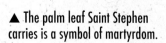

▲ Teresa wrote about her beliefs, which is why pictures often show her holding a quill pen.

Saint
TERESA OF ÁVILA

Even as a girl growing up in Spain Teresa seemed to be destined to devote her life to God.

When she was young she tried running away from home with her brother so they could be martyrs in Morocco, where Christians had been persecuted. Later she tried to be a hermit – living alone and spending her days praying – in the family's garden. At the age of 14, Teresa decided to become a nun, even though her father disapproved of her decision. He took some persuading, but eventually he had to accept that this was the life she had chosen. Teresa lived a simple life without any luxuries at all.

After around 25 years of being a nun, Teresa set up an order of nuns called the Discalced Carmelites – 'discalced' means that they were barefoot at all times like some of the earliest preachers hundreds of years before. Teresa's nuns followed her example – they lived simply and worked together as a team.

Lived:
1515–1582
Feast Day:
15 October
Patron saint of:
People who suffer
from headaches

▼ This convent was built on the site of Saint Teresa's birth.

MINOR SAINTS

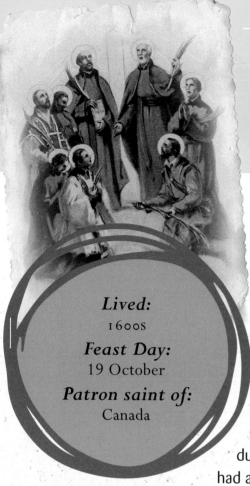

THE CANADIAN MARTYRS

Lived:
1600s
Feast Day:
19 October
Patron saint of:
Canada

The Canadian Martyrs were eight Jesuits priests, Fr Jean de Brébeuf, Fr Isaac Jogues, Fr René Goupil, Fr Antoine Daniel, Fr Jean de Lalande, Fr Gabriel Lalemant, Fr Charles Garnier and Fr Noël Chabanel who died while converting members of the native American Huron tribe in Canada. The priests were killed at various times during the 1600s at the hands of other tribes who had attacked the villages the priests were staying in.

KATERI TEKAKWITHA

Kateri Tekakwitha was canonised in 2012 and is the first Native American to become a saint. She was from the Mohawk tribe and became a Catholic when she was 19 years old, moving to a Jesuit village near Montreal. She led a life devoted to prayer, often fasting and making life deliberately uncomfortable for herself in an effort to feel closer to God. She died at the age of 24, but miracles have since been recorded in her name.

Lived:
1656–1680
Feast Day:
17 April (Canada);
14 July (USA)
Patron saint of:
Environment and ecology

Saint
THOMAS BECKET

Lived:
1118–1170

Feast Day:
29 December

Patron saint of:
Exeter College, Oxford University

Saint Thomas was one of Henry II of England's most trusted friends. As a young man he was quite extravagant – it was even claimed he had monkeys trained to ride horses alongside him when he went on journeys for the king. However, Thomas changed when he was made Archbishop of Canterbury. He lived a simpler life and disagreed with Henry on certain issues – which would lead to Thomas's death. Four knights, believing the king wanted Thomas dead, murdered the archbishop inside Canterbury Cathedral. Becket was made a saint in 1173 and many people made a pilgrimage to his shrine in Canterbury Cathedral.

▼ This image from the Trinity Chapel in Canterbury shows Thomas curing a sick man, one of the miracles he performed.

GLOSSARY

Apostle one of Jesus's original followers

Archangel an important, or chief, angel

Archbishop a high-ranking bishop in charge of other bishops

Baptise a ritual often performed to induct someone into a Christian church, it involves dipping someone into water or sprinkling them with water in a symbolic move to signify the washing away of impurity.

Beatify to announce that someone has led a good and holy life

Blasphemy insulting God

Canonise to make someone a saint

Convert to become a member of or change to a particular religion

Crucify to attach someone to a cross as a means of execution

Deacon someone who works as a preacher that is not as important as a priest

Feast day a special day of celebration

Gentile a non-Jew

Gospel the life and teachings of Jesus

Hermit someone who lives on their own, so they are not distracted from praying

Jesuit a member of the religious order the Society of Jesus

Martyr someone who dies for their faith or religion

Miracle a good event, often a medical cure, which cannot be explained by science

Missionary someone who travels to spread the word of God

Monk a male member of a religious order that live in their own community

Monastery a place where monks live

Nun a female member of a religious order that live in their own community

Patron someone who supports, protects or guides another person, people or an organisation

Persecute to treat someone badly or violently

Pilgrimage a visit to a holy place in order to pray, both at the place and on the journey

Preach/preacher spread the word of God/someone who spreads the word of God

Sacrifice to kill something as part of a religious celebration

Saviour a person who saves someone else; in Christianity another name for Jesus or God

Vatican the headquarters of the Roman Catholic Church

Viking traders and raiders from Scandinavia from the 8th–11th centuries

Further information

Websites

www.bbc.co.uk/education/topics/ztkxpv4/resources/1
www.bbc.co.uk/religion/religions/christianity/
www.catholic.org/saints

Books

A Year of Christian Festivals by Flora York, Franklin Watts, 2013
A Treasury of Saints by David Self, Lion Hudson, 2014
The Pope by Paul Harrison, Wayland, 2014
Mother Teresa by Paul Harrison, Wayland, 2016

INDEX